UNANIMOUS ANON
PRESENTS

LIV SLANIA
SUPERHEROICS
VOLUME ONE
A SHORT TEXTBOOK FOR MANKIND

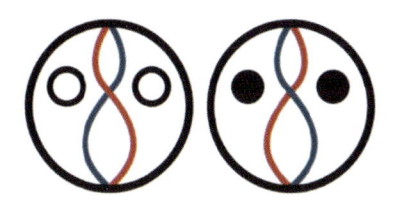

WE'RE LOOKING THROUGH CON GLASSES WHICH DIVIDE ALL THINGS
INSTEAD OF THROUGH **ONE** LENS THAT UNITES ALL BEINGS

DEDICATED TO ALL THE DREAMERS OUT THERE

2018

CODE RED

3, 2, 1.	7
PART ONE	10
PART TWO	16
PART THREE	24
PART FOUR	37
PART FIVE	42
PART SIX	48

CODE BLUE

PART SEVEN	62
PART EIGHT	67
PART NINE	71
PART TEN	77
FINAL THOUGHTS	87

"Tough times never last,
but tough people do."
- Robert H. Schuller

CODE RED

"Be an elf, not an ogre."

- Unanimous Anonymous

3, 2, 1...

Pssst, hey you, I'm talking to you! Now that I've got your attention, I'd like to begin by asking you a question. Which character would you say you have more in common with; a superhero or a supervillain, a friend or a foe, an elf or an ogre? I know that most of us would prefer to resemble an elf than an ogre, obviously, but I'd like you to please answer honestly, in just a few words, whether overall you feel more like a hero or a zero (the 'why' is always optional, for your own personal records).

_____

_____

Thank you. Let's proceed.

You're probably wondering, "What am I reading? What's going on here?" Well, in short, I'm a superhero cadet, and in order to graduate from the Superhero Academy I need to complete my final assignment. You know how all the different superheroes have numerous missions they go on? Well, this is officially my very first one; I've been given the task to help save humanity. "*How* are you going to do that?" you ask. That's simple, by letting you in on a little secret and showing you something called the Super Simple Moral Compass. This SSMC device is what all the superheroes and lead characters of sagas, legends and fairy tales live and, if needs be, die by on their journeys. It takes a lot of practice for each character (real or imaginary) to acquire the power of the compass by going through, and learning from, their many inner and outer battles of self-growth. Why? Because 'with great power comes great responsibility,' as quoted by Spiderman's uncle (Spidey credit goes to Stan Lee, of course).

I was meant to find you, you know. Now that I have, I may finally start fulfilling my mission as well as reigniting my, your and our calling. You ready? We're running out of time, so please take my verbal hand and go where, although you may never have been before, it feels like home. Yep, I'm literally about to give you the key of hope, but for this to work, you need to keep your mind and heart as open throughout this process as you can. Can you do that, please?

For both our sakes, I hope you will be able to remain focused on the end goal of this mission. The stakes are higher than ever, so don't let any preconceptions you may have hold you, or us, back. You're already good enough as you are and you're crucial for this world-saving plan to work (yes, really).

In case the virus (more about it later) kicks in and makes you think that you no longer want to keep on reading, let me first share some cliff notes from the textbook with you.

Imagine how many establishments would go out of business in a blink of an eye if, for example, people suddenly felt good about themselves and no longer needed all this material stuff to make them feel better. The reason why everyone is scared and unhappy instead of liberated and free is because your misery literally keeps making them money, and your obliviousness makes you easier for them to control. Oh, you don't know who *they* are? Yes, you do. It's those whose wars we keep on fighting, those whose words we keep on believing, and those whose taxes we keep on paying (mankind's the only species that pays to live on Earth).

> *"If you want to know who controls you,*
> *look at who you're not allowed to criticise."*
> - Voltaire

Because you've only just begun reading this, your attention span still wants to continue to see where this is going. A few exercises in, you will, however, be tempted to skip through them. One more or less doesn't make a difference, right? Wrong.

In order to build anything long-lasting, there's no skipping steps and no cheating of any sort. What you give, you get back.

> *"Without labour, nothing prospers."*
> - Sophocles

Let's first lay down the most basic, yet solid, fundamentals of superheroics (Volume One may, in places, sound very up or down, North or South; it does so for a reason). The end goal of this is for me to help you become a superhero (in your case, to be specific, a superhuman), which, in short, means you're incorruptible in all ways. Alongside this mission, we also need to gather all the other superhero cadets out there, one by one, help fine-tune them to the universal frequency of their true calling, and switch their (currently 'off') superhuman mode 'ON.' That includes you, too.

At the start of the course, as well as the superheroics textbook, every human cadet receives a copy of the humanual. It explains how to use the human vessel to which the cadet's soul has been assigned for the duration of their current life. Its message is very straightforward, that only truth will set you free. There is a catch, though. Well, *you* are the catch, because our journey together depends on the openness of your imagination (as does the future of mankind by the way, no biggie). Please stretch your mind to its limits, and keep the door of the 'possibility that I might (just might) be right' open.

3,2,1...

> *"Whatever is worth doing at all is worth doing well."*
> - Philip Stanhope, 4th Earl of Chesterfield

PART ONE

Since this is Volume *One* in the making here, it'd be handy for us to get the fundamentals out of the way. What/who is a superhero? It's a person who does good deeds. What do all superheroes have in common? They're all good. Regardless of their situations, superpowers, shortcomings, mistakes, looks, social ranks, pasts, fears or flaws, when push comes to shove, they simply continue to be, and do, good. Their paths are hard and filled with obstacles; they all suffer tremendous losses, pains and heartaches, but due to their incorruptible character, choose to unselfishly keep doing what's right. Why? Because:

a) nobody else will

b) you don't get a medal for just showing up.

How good are *you* then, hmm? It's nice being polite or well-mannered, but even Hitler was charismatic, loved children and dogs. That's not enough to call him a swell guy though, is it?

On the scale 1-10 (we call it the super scale), if 10 means 'super good,' how good would you say you are? (and the optional 'why')

_____

_____

On the 1-10 super scale, how honest would you say you are? ('why')

_____

_____

On the 1-10 super scale, how open-minded would you say you are? ('why')

___
___

Thank you.

Speaking of Hitler, he's just one of many examples in mankind's history where someone is trusted, followed, admired and supported by many all over the world. Now, what kind of place, reality and dimension would allow such leaders to lead the people? One which clearly needs urgent help.

If you think of the stories, books, films and tales you've grown up on, which one would you say the human world resembles more: The Shire or Mordor (JRR Tolkien credit)? Heaven or Hell? A fairy tale or a scary tale? ('why')

___
___

And if you think of all mankind as one species, would you say it behaves more like elves or ogres? ('why')

___
___

TABLE TIME

Below, I doodled a superhero table for you with some general adjective examples that describe all kinds of heroic characters:

THE SUPERHERO TABLE

GOOD	HONEST	BRAVE	LOVING
INCORRUPTIBLE	SELFLESS	GENEROUS	AUTHENTIC
HUMBLE	OPEN-MINDED	CARING	MORAL
FORGIVING	KIND	SUPPORTIVE	HELPFUL
GENUINE	UNDERSTANDING	RIGHTEOUS	ETHICAL

As you can see, I've left a few empty spaces for you to add any words if you'd like. Feel free to cross out any words you don't agree with, then keep on reading when you're happy with all the adjectives in all the columns.

Now, if you could please put a ✓ tick sign next to the adjectives, which describe you.

I suspect that you haven't ticked off all of the boxes, right? If so, that's OK because, as stated before, you are good enough. We haven't said that there's no room for improvement, though. There is, there always is, right? Please circle the correct answer.

Right

Wrong

Now we're going to do some maths together. I know this is really beginning to feel like school, but that's because it is (yey). The school system hasn't evolved for generations, so it'd be good to revamp it a little with the help of ethical teachings.

The original superhero table, without any changes you made, consists of 20 adjectives. Ticking all of them off would count as 20 out of 20 or, to simplify, 10 out of 10 on the super scale. If, for example, you've ticked off half of them, then it'd count as 5 out of 10 for team superhero within you. Can you calculate your result and jot down the score below?

DATE: _____
CURRENT SUPERHERO SCORE: _____

You know how at the start of any story, the lead character encounters something or someone giving them a choice which can, and does, influence their actions and impact the course of their lives? Well, our big moment is here, and I'm hoping my message will fill up your imagination. Nowadays, however, when everyone thinks they know it all, it's tricky to fill a cup that's already full. Instead of listening to one another, people get offended left and right, which only leads to more miscommunication and division (the two things we definitely do not need more of).

If everybody thinks they're the good guy though, how come there are all these bad things happening all around? Whose fault is it? Who keeps allowing the likes of Hitler to take charge and control of Earth's citizens? Does it sound like the behaviour of superheroes or supervillains? Elves or ogres?

Below is the super knowledge table with a few categories from the knowledge department:

THE SUPER KNOWLEDGE TABLE

HISTORY	BIOLOGY	ART	MUSIC
SCIENCE	SCIENCE FICTION	ASTRONOMY	ASTROLOGY
PHYSICS	METAPHYSICS	GRAPHIC DESIGN	SPORTS
PSYCHOLOGY	ARCHITECTURE	POLITICS	COMPUTERS
RELIGION	JOURNALISM	FASHION	CURRENT EVENTS

Same deal as the last table, empty slots for you to fill in, and freedom to cross out any you don't like. Once you're happy with the contents of the super knowledge table, please underline the topics that you have knowledge of.

Great. Now could you please put a ✓ tick next to the topics you have an opinion about? Do the ticks coincide with your knowledge by any chance?

What is 'knowledge,' anyway? Since knowledge is power, it must be important. The general definition of the word knowledge is: a familiarity with information, facts and skills, either a theoretical or practical understanding of a subject, attained through experience and/or education.

Can you please double-check the super knowledge table that you do, in fact, possess the knowledge of all your underlined subjects? If what you know about them fits the description of what knowledge is, please put a ◯ circle around the underlined word. If you feel you don't have the knowledge of that topic, please leave underlined.

Now, on the super scale (10 being 'super accurate'), how accurate would you say the ratio between your underlined and circled words is? ('why')

_____

_____

To save humanity, we need to replace the dysfunctional pieces of ourselves with healthy new ones, both as individuals and as a species. In order to know exactly which bits to replace, firstly we need to locate them. That's courage, and courage has many forms which include taking a hard look at yourself, your pros and cons, checking out the ratio between the two and working consciously towards improving that score.

Yes, so it might be scary, especially nowadays when people's relationship with truth seems passing at best. Nothing, however, will change the fact that all bubbles eventually burst and truth will never hurt as much as a lie, especially long term. If unsure, can you think of a superhero or a fairy tale character who has lied their way to happiness?

PART TWO

How do you know that what you think you know is correct? And how do you know that what others say they know is also correct? Who built your frame of reference? I mean, think about it. What's agreed to be the history of mankind is, in itself, a mix of some knowledge, some experience, some truths, lies, opinions, fears, prejudice and ignorance. Back in the day, the general access to information was very limited, therefore, populations remained uneducated for generations. Nowadays, however, there's no excuse for ignorance since, thanks to the internet, all the information (both right and wrong, true and false) is literally at our fingertips, accessible to a significantly larger percentage of people than ever before. That gives us the possibility to check any data and its sources.

Something doesn't add up, though. How come, that with all this access to knowledge, as well as the numerous social and scientific breakthroughs and advancements, we *still* don't know how to get along or how to be happy? Why not?

What's *really* stopping us from achieving peace and harmony on Earth? Do you think that peace is even possible? On the super scale (10 being 'super possible') how possible would it be to achieve peace on Earth according to you? ('why')

_____

_____

On the super scale (10 being 'super important'), how important is achieving peace on Earth to you? ('why')

_____

_____

We repeat what we don't repair. Since the history of mankind keeps repeating itself a lot actually, what does it tell you? Maybe it's obvious that humans keep making the same significant mistakes over and over, time after time, generation after generation? OK, well, it seems like the only way to move forward is to face these errors (human and otherwise), address them, learn from them and... make them no more. "Easier said than done," you say. Remember that if you do nothing - nothing happens, and if you change nothing - nothing changes, which directly applies to what, in superheroics, we call the four human superpowers:

1. Thoughts
2. Feelings
3. Words
4. Actions.

What we call 'imagination' is the most influential human superpower hidden inside us. It is the one power (superheroics calls it 'The Power Whole') which all the other four powers flow through and within.

BEFORE

Without giving you an unnecessarily long history lesson, I'd like for us to quickly travel through the past to brush up on our knowledge of our ancient forerunners.

ANCIENT MESOPOTAMIA (circa 3100BC - 539BC)
- (the Sumerians) invented the wheel and the first chariot
- (the Babylonians) invented the initial concept of maps (the Greeks and Romans further developed cartography)

- invented mathematics (the Egyptians then advanced a further numeral system for counting)
- developed a specific concept of time, dividing it into 60 parts (hence now we've got 60 second minutes and 60 minute hours)
- (the Sumerians) invented the very first calendar, dividing a year into 12 lunar months

Women: nearly equal to men, could trade, own land and divorce

ANCIENT EGYPT (circa 3100BC - 641AD)

- masters of the pyramids
- developed hieroglyphic writing on stone tablets then moved to papyrus and reed pen
- invented the mechanical clock and the first to use a 24 hour time period
- invented cosmetics and sophisticated methods of practicing medicine which mixed the natural (herbs and surgery) with the supernatural
- invented the phonetic alphabet where a symbol represents one sound and not a word

Women: had special rights, could own property, but could not rule in their own right or hold important positions, with a few exceptions

ANCIENT CHINA (circa 1600BC - 220AD)

- invented silk and paper
- invented movable type printing and created earliest printed money
- invented the compass

- invented gunpowder and fireworks
- the first to come up with ball games for entertainment

Women: inferior to men, faced discrimination, deprived of education

ANCIENT GREECE (circa 750BC - 146BC)

- advanced in art, science, theatre, poetry, geometry, astronomy, biology and architecture, also developed the concept of modern philosophy
- made the first alphabet with vowels (the word 'alphabet' comes from the two first letters alpha + beta)
- invented the Olympics
- Athens: the birthplace of democracy
- Sparta: a strictly ruled military state where individuality was put aside in favour of basic living and obedience

Women:

- in ancient Athens: uneducated, confined to their father's home, not allowed to walk freely around the city
- in ancient Sparta: literate and numerate, allowed to speak their minds and walk freely on the streets, had powerful status and respect, exercised, drove chariots

ANCIENT ROME (circa 753BC - 476AD)

- invented concrete, underfloor heating and built advanced aqueducts
- pioneered the use of the cesarean section
- invented the Roman alphabet and numerals, the first newspaper and made the first bound book

- developed a legal system used to this day as the basis for many European laws
- developed the concept of mass entertainment to keep their population distracted instead of rebellious; built the Colosseum, upon which present-day football stadiums are now modelled

Women:

- higher class: unable to work or act in their own interests, could inherit property but had no control over it, couldn't vote, speak out, hold important roles or attend political assemblies
- lower class: had to work for a living

ANCIENT MAYA (circa 2600BC - 1200AD)

- established the science of astronomy and the 365 day calendar system
- built structures such as galactic observatories and sanctuary pyramids
- discovered chocolate
- (although originated by the Olmec) the first ones to build ball courts
- built canals and straight roads

Women: could partake in administrative, economic and farming events, played a vital role in numerous rituals

ANCIENT AZTEC (circa 1300AD - 1521AD)

- the only civilisation to tax the rich and the nobles more than the poor
- invented popcorn and chewing gum
- one of the first civilisations to have mandatory education for boys, girls, rich and poor

- developed a form of hieroglyphic writing
- developed sustainable waste management and a thorough recycling system

Women: had some rights, could have paid jobs, their roles correlative to men

ANCIENT INDUS RIVER VALLEY (circa 3300BC - 1700BC)
- developed new techniques in handicraft, including seal carving
- one of the first ones to use buttons made of seashells, invented dice
- built oldest public bath houses and invented one of the first flush toilets; their homes were connected to a centralised sewage and drainage system
- the first ones to use public litter bins
- known for an exceptionally advanced form of dentistry

Women: treated with respect and dignity, some even held higher positions, but their main role was to bear children and take care of the household

ANCIENT PERSIA (circa 3000BC - 330BC)
- invented the art of letter-writing and developed a comprehensive postal system using relays
- invented the first refrigerator
- invented alcohol and discovered sulfuric acid
- created the first taxation system
- first global empire to be built on tolerance for other cultures
- the first ones to come up with a revolutionary concept of not enslaving subjects; Cyrus II (The Great) who, in the Bible, is called 'The Enlightened One,' freed Jews from Babylon

Women: equal to men, active members of society with social and legal freedom, made decisions together with men, praised for their conducts and not gender, free to marry whomever they wanted

After reading through these lists, could you jot down, in a few words, the first thing that comes to your mind?

_____

_____

Although these examples are literally the tip of the historical iceberg, this list alone makes for an impressive CV of the ancients. All the civilisations were clearly powerful, forward thinking, innovative, daring and ground breaking to unimaginable heights. That's all great, but why then have all of them fallen, ceased to exist and literally turned to dust? What's the common denominator between them all? Without them we certainly wouldn't be where we're at today, but we don't want to end up like them either, do we?

Imagine, if at their time, some of those civilisations had communicated, learned from one another and united instead of wasting so much time trying to conquer and to be in charge, where would we be now? If ancient Athens and Sparta had communicated with each other regarding even just *one* topic, for example, that of women's conditions, this interaction between the two states could've certainly saved us over two millennia of the oppression of women, aka the baby machines with no freedom of their own lives or bodies.

When we fast-forward through time until World War II, please picture where mankind could be now if the message of Hitler (yep, him again) had been one of equality and not oppression. Imagine what difference in the history of peace *one* more positive leader could make. No superhero would ever stand for, or support, violence, division, murder or pain of any kind, especially for one's own benefit. These are all supervillainous actions which leave us currently living in Gotham with no Batman anywhere in sight to save us (Batman credit goes to Bob Kane and Bill Finger).

> *"What is a good man but a bad man's teacher?*
> *What is a bad man but a good man's job?"*
>
> - Lao Tzu

PART THREE

Let's look at supervillains for a minute. On a storyline level, a supervillain is a 'once a goodie turned baddie' character, a foe with an unhappy life-story, as well as having a deep connection to the superhero, their direct opposite. When a superhero comes across any situation, they remain on the path of good (no matter how hard it is for them). A supervillain doesn't. Due to their pain, heartbreak or a traumatic event, a supervillain ends up doing bad things and hurting themselves and others instead.

Can you please write down your favourite superhero/supervillain combo? Why these characters in particular?

_____

_____

I've prepared a detailed supervillain table with various words describing a whole range of the villainous types:

THE SUPERVILLAIN TABLE

CONTROLLING	GREEDY	JEALOUS	HURTFUL	VENGEFUL	ANGRY
SELFISH	OPPRESSIVE	MEAN	RESENTFUL	EGOTISTICAL	JUDGEMENTAL
ENVIOUS	ENTITLED	AGGRESSIVE	MANIPULATIVE	SELF-SERVING	FEARFUL
INSECURE	VAIN	OPPORTUNISTIC	UNJUST	IMMORAL	COLD-BLOODED
MALICIOUS	CORRUPT	ARROGANT	RUDE	WEAK	CRUEL
HATEFUL	INCONSIDERATE	HOSTILE	UNETHICAL	RUTHLESS	VICIOUS
DESTRUCTIVE	CARELESS	UNCOMPROMISING	IRRESPONSIBLE	FORCEFUL	SUSPICIOUS

Can you please put a ✓ tick sign next to those adjectives which, even if only sometimes, describe you?

There's no need to calculate the score here because the point of this exercise is just to display that, regardless of your age, gender or social status, every human (literally every. single. one.) makes mistakes. The good news is that if everyone is a sinner then everyone can be a winner too. The bad news is that we are the common denominator between all the fallen civilisations (barring natural disaster, of course), and it's all our fault.

If you think of various movies or TV series, please choose a character you can relate to the most. Which other film/TV lead character(s) do you like? ('why')

_____
_____

If you and your life were turned into a TV series, would you like the personality, thoughts, words, feelings and actions of the lead character? Would you keep watching the series and root for them? Please write down your answer below. ('why')

_____
_____

"You are who you are
when nobody's watching."
- Stephen Fry

HUMANUAL A1

Every empire begins small, every journey has a start, and every lead character seems an unlikely superhero candidate until they begin to act accordingly.

In Volume One we focus on what can be improved within mankind right here and now, the everyday basics of superheroics. You know the saying, 'The devil's in the detail'? Well, those devilish details are what we're going to address next.

Let's look at the meaning behind the word 'supervillain' and analyse it again. In short: it is an unhappy person hurting those around them, with their own backstory that explains their behaviour, 'once a goodie turned baddie;' someone who reacts badly to bad things happening to them.

Below are some supervillain examples and their backstories in a nutshell:

BANE: rough childhood growing up within prison walls (DC Comics credit)

GOLLUM: was betrayed, then influenced and corrupted by the ring (JRR Tolkien credit)

DARTH VADER: did bad deeds to save the love of his life, got corrupted in the process (George Lucas credit)

JOKER: fell into a tank of chemical waste, disfigurement drove him insane (Bill Finger, Bob Kane and Jerry Robinson credit)

CATWOMAN: rough upbringing and very challenging life circumstances (Bill Finger and Bob Kane credit)

LEX LUTHOR: a car accident and the aftermath of complex life events (Jerry Siegel and Joe Shuster credit)

POISON IVY: seduced by a bad man who injected her with poison as an experiment, and drove her insane (Robert Kanigher and Sheldon Moldoff credit)

DOCTOR OCTOPUS: abusive childhood, trauma and guilt after the death of his mother (Stan Lee and Steve Ditko credit)

Knowing even a couple of details about their hardships makes it easier to understand and harder to judge them for their actions, doesn't it? Do their sufferings ring a bell by any chance? Can you relate at all? Do you know someone who can?

YES / NO

In superheroics, the main difference between a superhero and a supervillain is their reaction to:

PAIN:
- A superhero does good deeds, helps others even if they are suffering = selfless
- A supervillain, because they are suffering, hurts others too = selfish

JUSTICE:
- A superhero focuses on doing what's right = selfless
- A supervillain focuses on being right = selfish

SUCCESS:
- A superhero defines success by what they do = makes things happen = selfless
- A supervillain defines success by what they own = expects for things to happen = selfish

LOVE:
- A superhero says "I love YOU/I accept you and your ways" = selfless
- A supervillain says "Love ME/Accept me and my ways" = selfish

TIME:
- A superhero = patient = selfless
- A supervillain = impatient = selfish

LIFE:
- A superhero = optimist = sees good in others even if they don't see good in themselves = filled with gratitude = wants quality + peace = selfless
- A supervillain = pessimist = sees bad in others including those trying to help them = filled with guilt and regret = wants quantity + war = selfish

OTHERS:
- A superhero focuses on similarities = chooses unity despite differences = believes in 'stronger together' = selfless
- A supervillain focuses on differences = chooses division despite similarities = believes in 'each to their own' = selfish

How do *you* react when someone/something upsets you? How do you treat those who hurt you, whether they do it knowingly or not? I mean, it's easy to be nice to a nice person on a nice day in a nice place, right? Especially someone who:

a) can do something for you

b) can provide something that benefits you.

One's true character, however, shows its face in the 'not so ideal' case scenario called everyday life. It shows itself during rush hour, when one is running late, and/or in pain of any kind and in any situation. Mankind keeps failing at the little things which in superheroics are called 'Good Little Tests'.

HUMANUAL A2

The Good Little Tests (the GLTs) are sent to every person at the beginning of their 'video game' of life, and continue throughout all the chapters and levels that follow. Yes, so you may be 40 years old, but it also means you've reached level 40. Congrats!

The Good Little Tests consist of sometimes big, and sometimes small difficulties, obstacles, circumstances sent your way; a bad hair day, a traffic jam, the loss of someone you care about.

The small minus one points (-1s) are the tricky Good Little Tests that nobody seems to pay attention to. They are the bits we fail at, because we keep adding -1s here and there without realising that a) we're doing it and b) when we behave negatively it actually has an effect.

At the end of your current life, when your soul is in transition, your superhero and supervillain scores are counted. There are two options from then on. If you have managed to live a more superheroic life with a positive final score of the soul's existence, you move up. If, however, you end up living a more supervillainous life where your inner-ogre wins, your soul returns to have another go. It has to relearn everything from scratch with the hope that this time around it'll pass what it needs to in order to progress on its journey.

That's a pretty simple concept for our existence, wouldn't you say? Despite the moral map we've been given, in the matters of Good Little Tests, mankind still keeps going South in the ogre-direction instead. People get hurt when there is and when there isn't a reason to be (lose/lose situation). They get angry when there is and when there isn't a reason to be (lose/lose situation). They get jealous when there is and also when there isn't a reason to be (lose/lose situation again).

"There's no greater misfortune than having an enemy."
- Lao Tzu

"I don't like that man. I must get to know him better."
- Abraham Lincoln

If you hear someone saying bad things about you, perhaps you'll say: "Oh what a (insert a swearword of your choice)!" (-1). And you'll continue saying negative things in response: "Look how bad that person is!" (-1) / "Look what they've done!" (-1). Let me stop you right there. Is this a superhero or a supervillain talking back? When you say or do anything negative in return, you yourself become an ogre failing your Good Little Tests and adding -1s instead of +1s to the equation of your existence.

Well then, next time someone says or does something that offends you in real life/via social media, what are you going to do about it: behave like an elf (+1) or an ogre (-1)?

The times when most people lose their cool, become mean, aggressive and/or vengeful, *THAT* is when a superhero cadet activates their 'super' mode and focuses on: a) defusing the situation, b) defending peace.

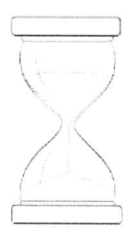

- You are assigned ONE sand timer per life with a limited amount of sand per person
- During that time, you come across a buffet of situations to teach you about the complete human experience
- Eventually, the sand runs out and your soul calculates the final super score
- Depending on whether + or − wins, your soul travels accordingly

- You are assigned ONE battery per life
- Sleep/rest recharges the battery to help operate the human vessel
- Eventually, it gets used up and recharges no more

If energy can neither be created nor destroyed, only be transferred or changed from one form to another (the First Law of Thermodynamics), then what about all those dying today, and from the past? Are their souls back on Earth? Are they still unfulfilled, damaged and hoping for better luck this time? How about those around you, have they reached happiness yet? If not, then each of the unhappy souls will have to return in the future and repeat this school grade all over again until they learn all of the lessons this level requires.

NUMBERS DON'T LIE

Looking at mankind mathematically for a moment, if we keep adding negative variables into the equation of humanity, whether willingly or not, independently we may be more destructive than we realise. Every single word or action changes the final result of the calculation, and if you think that you or your actions might be too small to make a difference, try sleeping with a mosquito (Dalai Lama's words).

Every morning, after recharging the batteries of your human apparatus and beginning from the neutral point **X**, you wake up and go empty yourself. Where does it go? Into nature (-1). You have your coffee/breakfast, plastic and packaging in action, and then, in the garbage can. Where does the rubbish go? Into nature (-1). You put a deodorant on, style your hair/fix your makeup, use some recyclable and some unrecyclable items, sprays here, wipes there. Where do they all go? Into the garbage can, and then, into nature again (-1). Therefore, before you've even left the house, you already owe nature back big time.

$$\leftarrow -10 \text{----} -5 \text{---} -1 \; \mathbf{X} +1\text{---} +5 \text{----} +10 \rightarrow$$

How the rest of the day goes (whether it's filled with +1s or -1s) depends entirely on you.

"Oh no, it's Monday." "Boo, it's raining." "It's too cold outside." "It's too hot today." "This is wrong." "That isn't right." "Those are awful." Do any of these ring a bell to you? People nag, judge, whine, complain, whinge, criticise and nit-pick all day, every day, week, month, year, until they perish. So you know, you can't have a fairy tale ending with a bitter heart, for if you keep adding negative variables into your equation, your result will always be a negative one.

Can you imagine a chimp sitting on a tree, peeling a banana and thinking, "Life's so unfair! If *only* I had wings, I'd be happy!" Or an eagle flying above that chimp and contemplating, "Life's so unfair! If *only* I had thumbs, I'd be happy!" In nature, have you ever seen an anorexic elephant or an obese giraffe? Ever heard of zebras engaged in a never-ending bloody battle with the gazelles to find out who owns that piece of savanna? Or a wolf commanding other wolves to eliminate all the bears for being the inferior species? No? Why do you think that is? Well, maybe because a) everything in nature has its place, and b) unlike humans, animals live in harmony with their environment? Maybe we really are the only ones running in circles and destroying Earth along the way? Nature doesn't make mistakes. We do.

Who was it that actually placed humans at the apex of the planet's hierarchy pyramid? Oh, it was us. We literally crowned ourselves Kings of the World, and haven't questioned it since. Well, let's ask ourselves now, shall we? What have we done exactly to justify claiming that highest spot or the fact we feel entitled to the world's belongings as if they were our property? Why do we use the whole earthly source of life as our personal resource? What type of character in any story takes everything for themselves, places the crown on their head and goes, "Mine! It's all mine!"? A superhero or a supervillain? An elf or an ogre? A goodie or a baddie?

Now... Which one are *you*?

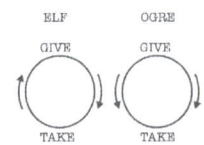

ELF   OGRE
GIVE   GIVE
TAKE   TAKE

VIRUS

As we're all perfectly aware, nobody enjoys being told they're in the wrong. To save humanity from yet another self-destruction we must, however, admit that we are the problem, both together *and* individually.

SUPERVILLAIN IS BAD WHEN UNHAPPY + MANKIND IS ALWAYS UNHAPPY (look around you, there's always pain somewhere in the world)
= MANKIND IS ALWAYS A SUPERVILLAIN

Both our time and energy in this world are limited, and the clock is ticking. When you use your time and energy for something bad, you're then left with less energy and less time to do something good. It's not a 'maybe.' It's logic.

> *"Gold rings and necklaces are easy to obtain in this world.*
> *A heart of gold, however, is the real treasure."*
> - Unanimous Anonymous

> *"No beauty shines brighter than that of a good heart."*
> - Shanina Shaik

People have tried to find ways of keeping humans on the right track. There have even been suggestions to get rid of money, as it (and the love of it) has been named the 'root of all evil.' Nice thought, but money in itself is meaningless. It's the worth and importance that we put on the value of money which matters. Therefore, if money disappears, there will be something else in its place leading us astray. Why? Because humans are infected with a severe virus, the dictator of mankind's wrong-doings and wrong-goings. It's called consuma virus, and you're infected too.

If you don't take control of your mind, someone else will, and if you stand for nothing you'll be more likely to fall for anything. In the consuma society of too much, there are plenty of 'anythings' for you to fall for, including a multitude of temptations designed to control you. It's worth keeping in mind that only uninformed people follow public opinion and the informed ones make up their own minds by gaining knowledge and doing research. Why? First of all, it's not good to follow the masses because lately, more often than not, the 'm' is silent! Second of all, because info without research is a rumour and rumours are carried, spread and accepted by the unquestioning, which is not very superhero-like, is it?

The reason you, I and others are infected with the virus is because we're the product of it. How does it work? Oh, it's a slick and clever little bug corrupting us inside and out. In order to remain undetected, it clouds people's minds and alters their senses as well as their values. Apart from the fact we're breathing consumair all around us, individually it also works through con glasses (CGs). The CGs are invisible, but sit comfortably on your face, busy distorting your reality and making you prone to abusing all the superpowers assigned to you. Out of all the living things on Earth, humans are the only ones infected.

These con glasses look favourably upon con men/women. In fact, they look favourably upon the act of con itself, for that's the virus in full motion. A con man/woman is someone who tricks and convinces others to believe something that's not true. Therefore, a lie, any lie, equals a con of sort. Looking through our past, I'd even dare say that con artist is the oldest profession in our history, since mankind's rises and falls have involved lying, cheating and deceiving one another.

On the super scale (10 being super often), how often do you:

a) say things that aren't true? ('why')

_____

_____

b) say things that aren't true for your personal gain? ('why')

_____

_____

> *"We join spokes together in a wheel, but*
> *it is the centre hole that makes the wagon move.*
> *We shape clay into a pot, but*
> *it is the emptiness inside that holds whatever we want.*
> *We hammer wood for a house, but*
> *it is the inner space that makes it liveable."*
>
> - Lao Tzu

PART FOUR

In superheroics, there's no time off from doing the right thing. Happiness is the way, right? But how do we get onto that happy road, then? Where is it and where does it start? Well, this is it, you and I right here today, clearing the path to happiness. Yes, there will be mistakes along the way, but don't get discouraged. Just ask yourself a) what, in your view, needs to happen for you to hit that 'happiness' target, b) calculate how much you believe in the possibility of getting there. I'm asking, because a) what you believe you receive, and b) if you don't have a goal to move towards, you settle for where things are.

Always remember that you have a choice to do nothing. As we previously mentioned, if you do nothing - nothing happens, and if you change nothing - nothing changes. There's no way to excuse or wriggle yourself out of this one. 'If you change the way you look at things, the things you look at change.' (Wayne Dyer credit). Instead of seeing a glass half empty, you can choose to see it half full. You can also choose to find out whether you can or cannot see beyond your nose in a world that's divided into wealth and privilege for a few, and poverty and oppression for the rest.

You may think that what's happening across the ocean, the continent or the border doesn't concern you, but it is all happening around the corner from us. Just because humans are small doesn't mean the world is big. It isn't. Nonetheless, most of us are preoccupied within our own bubble, and so we're utterly indifferent about what's happening beyond. It's typical of mankind to only pay attention to their individual needs whilst ignoring the rest. "Not my problem," we often say. It's time for us to realise that doing the bare minimum isn't enough for us to justify our existence. It isn't sufficient for you to take care of yourself and your close ones without a single care for the rest. "As long as my kids and I are alright, I don't care." Would you say that sounds like a goodie or a baddie talking?

We're acting this way because we're comfortable, and comfort is the number one enemy of progress. What a predicament we've found ourselves in.

THE WORLD

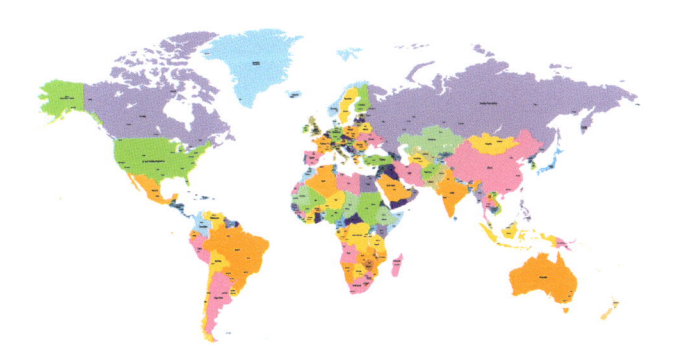

Can you please put an X on the map of the world, the place where you live? How about your close family? And your extended family? Your friends? Colleagues? Classmates etc?

On the super scale (10 being super often), how often would you say you impact those around you on a daily basis? ('why')

_____

_____

On the super scale (10 being super often again), how often would you say you impact those around you positively on a daily basis? ('why')

_____

_____

Two centuries ago, in 'The Parable of The Madman', Fredrik Nietzsche wrote: "God is dead. God remains dead. And we have killed him. How shall we comfort ourselves, the murderers of all murderers? What was holiest and mightiest of all that the world has yet owned has bled to death under our knives: who will wipe this blood off us?"

His big concern was that without God or a god-like symbol in our lives, there is no purpose for us as well as no authority figure for our ethical principles. What Nietzsche predicted would follow the post-Christian era is the disorder of cultural preferences and the excess of individual choices, all trying to fill that void within us.

Nietzsche also foretold that people would quit being curious and stop asking relevant questions due to their new 'religion of comfortableness.' He said their concerns would be fixated on the petty things full of irrelevant, unimportant, vain, hollow and self-conceited blankness; thus making people extra busy, and compensating by fooling themselves that their empty and mediocre lives make them happy.

"Many a man thinks he is buying pleasure,
when he is really selling himself to it."
- Benjamin Franklin

Would you say you are the type of person who is driven by their dreams or their fears? ('why') Also, imagine if fear was no longer part of your life, what do you think you'd be doing differently? ('why')

_____

_____

"Because I have known despair, I value hope.
Because I have tasted frustration, I value fulfilment.
Because I have been lonely, I value love."
- Leonard Nimoy

GOOD AND BAD

In your life, some know you as (insert your name) _____ the Good. Some know you as (insert your name) _____ the Bad. Some know you as both, but choose to see the good. And vice versa. On some days, to some people you're great (passing the Good Little Tests with positive variables), then on some other days you're not so great because of this or that. There are those who stick by you despite the ogre-ness within you, and there are those who will run because of it.

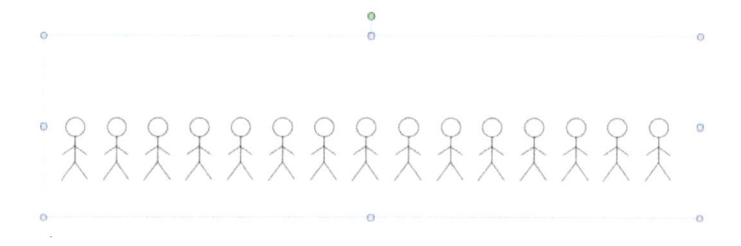

This stick figure picture represents mankind. At least one of them is white, another one black, one of them is Muslim and another, Buddhist, there is a man and a woman in there, a transgender person, someone straight as well as gay, an elder and a child. Which one of them offends you the most? The superhero cadet's answer would be 'none, because we're all the same and the rest is irrelevant.'

> *"Any situation that you find yourself in, you decide which route to take:*
> *North or South/good or bad. If you're trying to get North*
> *but you keep walking South, you shouldn't be surprised*
> *why you're not at your desired destination yet."*
> - Unanimous Anonymous

PART FIVE

We all need a dentist or a doctor in our lives. Some think everyone needs a spiritual or a political guru. People could, however, also benefit from having someone take care of their public image, a public relations (PR) press officer of sort. Why do we all need one? Because every single one of us ultimately depends on their reputation for survival, success and acceptance. And we don't realise it.

Superheroics focuses on the super public relations of individuals to then help their souls progress towards insight. That's the goal in a nutshell, always doing the right thing and always being a good person, as close to that superhuman ideal as possible and the most honourable you can be in all ways. Oh, and with the con glasses off, there's no such thing as 'what's right for me may not be right for you,' because right is right = the incorrupt way, and wrong is wrong = the corrupt way, always.

Word of mouth is the most powerful source in public relations. Every chat, every declaration, every sentence, tweet, share, article, whisper, phone conversation, text is word of mouth, just in different forms. Here's the thing. You're your own PR person, your own self-representative. Are you doing a good job within the role assigned to you?

In the consuma society filled with con infected ogres, you can't expect anyone to 'take your word for it' just because you say so. In order for people to respect you, you need to earn their respect by proving you deserve it. By behaving like an elf and not an ogre, and by doing your PR appropriately, if someone smears your name, it won't be believed (or at least it'll be believed much less). If you act like a superhero, the truth will eventually prevail. The only way for it to work is if you lead by example because 'fine words butter no parsnips.'

CIRCLE

Would you be so kind as to draw a circle below? (yep, a simple circle)

Great. Now, could you please draw a circle the other way? (if you drew it anti-clockwise above, please draw clock-wise below)

Next, compare the two circles and see if you can notice a significant difference between them (i.e. that the first circle you've always drawn this way since you were able to hold a pencil, whilst the other one was your first attempt to draw it differently).

Is it fair to say that quality-wise they are both more similar than not? What does this tell us? Maybe that just because we're used to doing something a certain way, it doesn't necessarily mean it's the only, the most efficient or even the correct way to do it? And how come that all these years you haven't tried to draw a circle the other way around? Just to try it, you know? Do you not question what you're taught, but simply conform and obey? Do you not try new methods of imagining, doing, thinking, feeling, being? Sure, you're more likely to make mistakes that way, but the one who never makes mistakes doesn't create anything new either. You can't be both safe and brave, not when it comes to the superhero cadet's journey towards truth.

Let's look at our search for truth in a new way, with the con glasses off and one lens of unity on, outside the box, like the new circle drawing way. What if we firstly lay down a map indicating our end goal to then understand the route to get there? If you don't know where you're going, how are you supposed to know the next step? Whatever you do, you always want the best version of yourself to prevail. It's important to remember that in superheroics, the meaning of the word 'best' equals better than 'good,' not more: rich, successful, fit, famous. Therefore, 'your best' simply means you being as turbo-good as you can be (such as the way you behave towards someone you care about).

In order to get closer to that goal, it's worth double-checking if all the thoughts and feelings within you are still valid, because more often than not, you'll find yourself thinking or feeling on auto-pilot (as you've done so for years). You wouldn't eat expired food, so why waste time on expired opinions? It's these backward ways which lead to divisions made of labels and stereotypes. The only good thing about knowing which stereotype describes you is being aware of what image you're up against. And whichever stereotype you are, be a good one (blonde stereotype, nerdy stereotype, sporty stereotype, famous stereotype etc). All stereotypes focus only on a shell of a human body, which is what people see when they look at you. The remaining 99% of what makes you 'you,' is the part that remains hidden away in your head for the majority of your life. Have you ever realised that the 'mind-drive' where you store the entire realm of your imagination never sees the light of day? Why not?

CHILDREN

Children are our future. Obvious, right? Well, if that's really the case, then why do we keep raising kids who need to recover from their childhoods when they grow up? By the time they're semi-functional, they're old, and then soon after, they're dead.

When it comes to mankind's education system, it hasn't evolved much for over a century. The old school traditions, apart from the knowledge, also include racism, homophobia and bullying, even in kindergartens. Why is that? How is that? Who keeps teaching all these bad and ogre-like morals to the new generations?

> *"When a child comes into your life,*
> *it is time to relearn life,*
> *not teach them your ways."*
> - Sadhguru

Right, let's look at the essence of what we know about children:
1. They are not conscious of any division between people and will play with anyone until an adult tells them not to.
2. They do not differentiate between facts or fiction, art or science, history or bedtime story, no boundaries of any kind. To them, everything is information, and information is everything.
3. They do not give up when learning new things, for if they gave up as easily as the adults do, we'd be walking on all fours for the rest of our lives.

4. They do not need to think outside the box, because the box hasn't, as of yet, been created in their free-flowing and unlimited imagination.
5. They observe the grown-ups, believe all they see, then process, learn and mirror it back.

Small children aren't as affected by the consuma virus simply because they haven't been exposed to it for as long as the grown-ups have. While you may be thinking it's too late for you to be a superhero, what if you help raise one instead? There's nothing wrong with being a super sidekick like Alfred, Fairy Godmother or Mufasa (credit to Batman's and Disney's teams). Yes, the characters may be fictional, but their values are very real, noble, truthful and timeless.

When kids watch films or cartoons, they don't focus on the wealth or the looks only (not until they hear grown-ups pin-pointing those); they focus on the bravery and superheroism of the characters, and get inspired to be like them. Kids are meant to make up their own minds about the world they're growing up in, but what happens instead is that the parents make up the kids' minds for them; not only with facts or good advice, but with con virus affected opinions, traumas, aches and fears. We know how susceptible children are to what the adults say, and when they keep hearing, "Batgirl isn't real" (Bill Finger and Sheldon Moldoff credit), "Superman doesn't exist" (Stan Lee credit), they simply stop believing in magic, unity, bravery and good virtues. As they're growing up, instead of following their dreams, they turn into gold junkies, get caught up in the chase for the dollar-covered holy grail, and just like that, the con virus claims yet another victim. It's that simple.

"You can now fake to look like a superhero,
but you can never fake being one."
- Unanimous Anonymous

PART SIX

If it sounds like a cow, acts like a cow and looks like a cow, it probably is a cow. Now, how about if it sounds like an ogre, acts like an ogre but looks like an elf? Our con culture is a spectacle of illusions. Why? In the consuma society, almost everyone is caught up with the matters of appearance, all wanting to look like their favourite pop star, film star, model, football star, fantasy character and so on. It's impressive to what extent some people go in order to achieve the look they want. That, however, cons others into believing that those who look good, rich, famous or fit are confident and happy. By now, we must know that's not the case (think of all the celebrities ending their lives and everyone's shocked, saying: "What? He/she was unhappy? But they were so famous and so rich!") and, in fact, see it's the consuma virus talking.

Are you one of those who complain about their appearance?

YES / NO

Would you look better or worse if, instead of your exterior, people could see your character instead? Please jot down the answer ('why').

_____

_____

"It is amazing how complete is the delusion
that beauty is goodness."
- Leo Tolstoy

True freedom and independence don't care for looks, popularity or a flat tummy, but for matters of the soul, invisible to the eye. Once the con glasses are off, the picture becomes pretty straightforward. Want to be a superhero? Act like one instead of only trying to look like one. Looks are deceiving, and it's time we stopped being this vain.

Keeping in mind that a) you won't influence mankind by trying to be like it and b) you have to be odd to be number one, let's for a moment forget all we've been taught and look at the world through children's eyes, with the con glasses off, and by going back to basics with the help of an RTI scan. The Return To Innocence scan only focuses on the very core of the information/the root of the message; no semantics, sub-details, sub-differences, sub-cultures or sub-extras of any kind. Once the fundamentals are laid out, we can move forward, and those fundamentals are:

Unity = good/elf/superhero
Division = bad/ogre/supervillain

Let's put all our ancient ancestors in one super bucket now (no con glasses separation) and notice they all achieved greatness. Some did it without a wheel or running water, others without any efficient means of communication, medicine and most things we know or have around us today. Yet they all did pretty well for a period. In order for us not to follow in their ill-fated footsteps, let's begin by looking at the common objectives running across the minds of emperors, pharaohs, kings and queens. Power, wealth and glory seem to be the main themes in literally every time and place throughout the history of mankind. Based solely on that fact alone, it's pretty clear those particular goals cannot be the right goals for humanity to have.

Do these goals seem more superheroic or supervillainous to you? ('why')

_____
_____

In our present-day society, we've progressed in so many ways than ever before. It would be a big shame to have to begin from scratch all over again once it all falls apart (it's happening as you're reading this, and the clock is ticking). Mankind is in serious danger. It doesn't need to be, though. You and I are here to save it, right?

*"You may not control
all the events that happen to you,
but you can decide not to be reduced by them."*
- Maya Angelou

REAL LIFE SUPERHERO = THE MASTER

We already know that all the superheroes/fairy tale characters represent those that are good and do good things, regardless of anything negative happening to them. In our society, being 'good' is a superpower in itself since the majority of people act and react like ogres based on their past misfortunes; not unity or bravery based on their dreams. Despite that, however, many men and women have lived by their unbreakable superheroic values. We've got countless admirable examples in history, such as Martin Luther King Jr, Albert Einstein, Maya Angelou, Mahatma Gandhi, Bob Marley, Muhammad Ali, Beatrix Potter, Tupac Shakur, Nelson Mandela, Eleanor Roosevelt and the list goes on, with more individuals whose morals and love for mankind were of the utmost importance to them.

> *"The Master views the parts with compassion*
> *because he understands the whole.*
> *His constant practice is humility.*
> *He doesn't glitter like a jewel,*
> *but lets himself be shaped by The Tao (the Way),*
> *as rugged and common as stone."*
>
> - Lao Tzu

I'd like to add a few more names in one super bucket: Buddha, Moses, Jesus and Muhammad (remember please, no con glasses separation, one lens only). Putting the older religious writings aside and focusing on the similarities between their teachings, these men all said the same thing, just in different words: be good, be truthful, be respectful, be brave, do what's right no matter what, put others' needs above your own fears, care for your soul, live in balance and harmony with others, and love without limit.

Now, how can anyone argue with that message? *How?* These are exactly the same values that any superhero, from Wonder Woman (credit to DC Comics) to a Care

Bear (credit to Those Characters From Cleveland/TCFC), lives by. What all the superheroes have in common, apart from being good, is that they're all incorruptible too. How about you then? On the super scale (10 being super incorruptible), how incorruptible would you say you are? ('why')

_____
_____

Before we go any further, we need to learn about our place in this world. There are many people out there wanting to make a difference, trying to help nature. We can see their results beginning to show, from cleaner beaches to animal conservation, and overall more eco-friendly decisions.

"Never discourage anyone who continually makes progress, no matter how slow."

- Plato

*"How wonderful it is that nobody need wait a single moment
before starting to improve the world."*

- Anne Frank

ECO AND EGO

Next, you have two diagrams waiting for you. The one to your left shows how mankind sees themselves; on top of the pyramid, better than everyone and everything else. The one to your right represents the truth.

```
EGO         ECO
  Human       Human
   /\          ◯
  /  \
 /____\
```

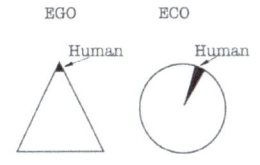

We're a part of the circle of life, a literal piece/component of the pie/ π which consists of:

a) the world
b) the world's family
c) the universe.

It's time for us to act like reputable Earth family members because we don't want to be that irritatingly problematic relative everyone dislikes at a gathering, right? Well, we are that relative, and from the moment we joined the Earth family's dinner table, many species have died and become extinct due to our irresponsible behaviour.

Last century seemed dedicated to attacking, persecuting and murdering the Jews. Then it was the Muslims' turn. Who's next? Who decides who's next? Let's go back in history to the times of Henry VIII who not only famously chopped his wives' heads off, but also divided the Church literally in half. What followed? His son Edward took over the throne, and started hacking at the Catholics. That didn't go down very well. Then it was Edward's sister Mary's turn. She, on the other hand, began murdering the Protestants. That also didn't bring a fairy tale ending. Next came the youngest of the siblings, Elizabeth I, who allowed both the Catholics and Protestants to co-habit, as well as jointly defend England from Spain, united against a common enemy. And guess what? In British history, that era was called the Golden Age in which Queen Elizabeth I reigned for over 44 years.

STRONGER + TOGETHER + ALWAYS = TEAM

My point with the last example is to show you that by accepting each other we are stronger together, as opposed to being divided. Look at WWII's Operation Dynamo where many private citizens in their 'little boats' mobilised towards one common cause and managed to assist the Navy in saving 300,000 troops at Dunkirk. Can you see there's strength in numbers? Together, we can achieve sensational things.

Since, scientifically speaking, the only reality you know is your own perception of it, then who's to tell you that you're not Batman/Wonder Woman, or anyone you wish to be? Who's to tell you that there's no way for you to be happy? And who's to tell us that it's not possible for mankind to live in peace? Impossible is nothing, not a thing.

"It always seems impossible until it's done."
- Nelson Mandela

"The road to progress and Enlightenment is a marathon that continues on until the very last runner crosses the finish line."
- Unanimous Anonymous

Let's briefly look at the Star Wars superheroic characters (credit to George Lucas) and the Avengers (credit to Marvel and Disney). In these two examples, the individuals are different from each other, looks and personality-wise, but they're a team, working together for a good and honourable cause. That's the power of team spirit, right? It'd be much easier for mankind to progress if we made the effort to see each other as members of a team, and not the current supervillainous 'each to their own' attitude.

Yes, mankind is a team, ONE team, and every team is only as strong as their weakest member.

CODE BLUE

Below, I've prepared a list for you with a few human weakest link potentials. Please have a read through them and underline only the one which, according to you, is the very weakest link and in need of our most urgent help:

the homeless
the starving
the orphaned
the mistreated/oppressed
the mentally ill/depressed/suicidal
the unemployed
the poor
the old/young
the alcoholics/addicts
the refugees

_____

_____

On the super scale (10 being super difficult), how difficult was it for you to pick just one from the list above? ('why')

_____
_____

Thank you.

OUR CORNER OF THE UNIVERSE

"New Earth is ready for Its final rebirth,
the soon awakened army of warriors
with a 20/20 vision towards It.
It is everywhere and It is Love,
It is Faith and It is Truth.
When you provide me with your three Its
'Eye/I' will provide the rest."

\- The Source

Let's keep all human beings in one super bucket still (no con glasses division). Reaching beyond the financial status, housing situation, mental and physical health, gender or skin colour, you will see that all of us have the potential to become that weakest link. Why? Due to the simple fact that everyone is suffering. Yes, whoever you can think of, they're surely worried, nervous, stressed out and concerned about something; from the rich, the poor, the abused, the abusers, to the employers, the employees, the young, the old, men, women, transgender, gay, straight, black, white, tall, short, you, we, everyone.

We live in a society where money is medicine, but no matter how much money one has, the whole of mankind is sick. Maybe that's because it's a con medicine, and we need an entirely different prescription? Maybe money is just a means to an end, but not an answer to all of our problems? We already know that children, plants or animals wouldn't be running after money out of choice. Neither would the non-con humans, elves or superheroes. Those with money would also use it for the good of others.

GRATITUDE EQUATION

Many people have:

no home
no job
no money
no education
no food/water
no electricity
no healthcare
no freedom
no peace
no love

The Gratitude Equation calculation is easy. You simply add +1 next to each thing on the list that you have. Can you fill in the score below?

THE CURRENT GRATITUDE EQUATION SCORE: ___ / 10

"Fame or integrity: which is more important?
Money or happiness: which is more valuable?
Success or failure: which is more destructive?"

- Lao Tzu

"Nowadays, people feel so entitled that, without the will to put in effort or work,
they expect for things to come to them just because they say so.
And these are the same people who say they don't believe in magic."
- Unanimous Anonymous

PART SEVEN

When I was helping The (Real) Author with preparing one of the superheroics chapters at our HQ one evening, Monday showed up unexpectedly and, when hearing what we were up to, insisted on giving a quote: 'I work once a week between Sunday and Tuesday. My shift lasts 24 hours. During that time, however, numerous people abuse me by blaming me for the fact they're late for work, tired after the weekend and/or unhappy with their overall existence. I just want them to know that I'll keep showing up to do my part, and I'd like for them to focus on doing theirs, instead of wasting their time complaining once a week for nothing. One day they're gone, game over and no more Mondays. Would they prefer that?'

Apart from mankind's infamous finger-pointing tactics, Monday has got another important message here; a gentle reminder that neither the weekdays nor the weather, the world, the seasons or the traffic revolve around you and your personal schedule. Therefore, you can't blame it for anything. The world keeps on going, yet we, instead of going along with it, declare war upon it.

What's our problem? What's yours? Do you know? Before we keep blaming God or yet another Monday for anything bad going on in our lives, we first need to ask ourselves: Why do we need a powerful entity such as God in order for us to *not* make the wrong decisions? Can't we make the right ones on our own? Are we that mindless? I mean, right is right even if no one is doing it, wrong is wrong even if everyone is. The moment we use our common sense, the path becomes very straight, simple and clear. In short, the only way is up but without an invisible force preventing any of us from making future mistakes. Why not? Because that's what having the freedom of choice is about.

SUPERHEROES WIN
SUPERVILLAINS LOSE

♥

No matter how good looking, rich or powerful they are, baddies always end up miserable. Can you think of any supervillain who's had their 'happy ever after'? I'm going to guess no. So if you make supervillainous choices in your life, you're 99.9% more likely to end up unhappy. If, however, you make superheroic choices, with patience you will get there. Superheroic means living and achieving your goals with a clear conscience because that's the only way your soul can actually move upwards.

Our free will doesn't force us to do bad things, but (as it says on the package) gives us the freedom to decide. When we happen to make the wrong choice, however, instead of admitting it, we let our con skills of deception and trickery work their magic at covering up the truth instead. Which part of 'only truth will set us free' do we not understand? If/when you're unsure of what to do next, just ask yourself: What would Batman/Wonder Woman/a <u>trustworthy</u> person do in your situation?

        Those who call themselves Christian, Muslim, Buddhist, religious, spiritual, open-minded or understanding must not be judgmental, racist, fascist or patronising in any way. Well, that's not quite how it is, is it? Instead of following in the peaceful footsteps of Buddha, Jesus, Abraham, Moses or Muhammad, many of these so-called believers argue, judge, fight and kill one another because, for example, some men call God "Jahveh" and others call God "Brahma."

        Here's where a very hypocritical scenario comes in. Since none of the preachers spoke of murdering each other like barbarians, why do so many of us behave contrary to their philosophies? In our society, greed tramples beliefs since there's no money to be made in peace, and instead of doing what's right, certain powerful people prefer to keep this turmoil of division going.

        Can you tell me why so many seem so quick to mock the names and teachings of these holy men? It's not their fault that their names are used as an excuse to justify some people's actions. Would you insult Batman/Wonder Woman if someone committed atrocities in their name? No? Why insult The Enlightened Prophets, then? In fact, why insult anyone at all? What would a superhero or an elf do in this situation? They'd do what's right; they'd appreciate these spiritual men and their legacies by helping to bring peace between their followers. What they wouldn't do is disrespect them.

Science and religion have been unable to co-exist side by side, so maybe we could try to unite them? Let's take the creation of the universe in seven days as an example. Some perceive this message literally, i.e. seven twenty-four hour cycles. Others don't. That'd be OK (we're free to believe what we choose) if both sides weren't at each other's throats, mocking one another and bickering over who's right.

Why not connect the two sides to the same story instead? To us, one day is nothing. To a little mayfly, it's their entire life. Therefore, to an infinite and everlasting God, millions of years are exactly what one day is to little us. The story of our universe makes sense both scientifically (body, literal) and spiritually (soul, symbolic), so what's the issue?

What is our well-being actually worth? Does the price vary depending on the skin colour or belief system by any chance? How much more will it cost us until we start paying attention before it's too late? Which part of 'we're all equal' is unclear?

BLOOD CELL = YOU   YOUR BODY = EARTH

Imagine yourself as a tiny little red blood cell inside a human body. There you are, wandering around some dark vein-tunnels, minding your own business, not knowing why you're there or what's what. Then you come across a bunch of other red blood cells beating up a white blood cell because of its colour. You keep on going and next you witness one lung stealing all the oxygen from the other lung. Then you notice the brain declaring war on the heart, because each of them thinks that they are the highest power within this human body. You keep drifting around on your journey, when suddenly you see another group of red and white blood cells having a full on fight. You hear them insulting one another and getting more and more violent. Why? Because the red cells believe the human is called Jack, but the white cells believe that the human's name is Ben.

How long do you think a human body could sustain itself if such conflict within it were the case? Not long, but that's exactly what we're doing to our world, so how much longer do you think it will sustain itself? This is supposed to be our home, our own corner of the universe, right? Apparently not. Thanks solely to us, Earth's becoming a lethal wasteland instead.

"In harmony with the Tao (The Way),
the sky is clear and spacious
the earth is solid and full
all creatures flourish together
content with the way they are
endlessly repeating themselves
endlessly renewed.
When man interferes with The Tao (The Way),
the sky becomes filthy
the earth becomes depleted
the equilibrium crumbles
creatures become extinct."

- Lao Tzu

We want to travel through space and time. What else? We want to be immortal, live on the Moon, Mars and other worlds, realms plus dimensions. Luckily for everyone, mankind can't do that yet (getting closer, though). Why? Because, as populations keep advancing, all we bring with us is the invasive 'con mind-set.' We've polluted our world and now want to escape elsewhere. We can't do the 'out of sight, out of mind' game any longer.

So... Be the good guy/gal! I mean, look around you. You *are* as good as Earth gets, and your home is calling you to help save it once and for all! The final insurgency against ogres (both inner and outer) and the reunification of elves is imminent. It's your choice whether you want to be part of the solution or do nothing, thus remaining part of the problem. Finding one's way with the help of superheroics is a safe route to take. It's not the easiest one (quite the contrary for it stands directly against the consuma virus), but one leading to balance.

On the super scale, how important is achieving peace on Earth to you? ___ / 10

Can you please compare your current score with the one on page 17 (the first time this question popped up)? Thank you.

> *"Let there be peace on Earth,*
> *and let it begin with me."*
> - Edgar Mitchell

PART EIGHT

What if I told you that we're all born geniuses, but life de-geniuses us, would you believe me? What if I added it was a respected philosopher, theorist and architect Richard Buckminster Fuller who'd actually said it? Would you believe him and have more faith in yourself? Although I'd really like for you to answer 'yes,' I doubt you'd take it to heart and say with conviction, "I AM a genius!" The thing about the majority of people is that they also don't think they're one either.

Since everyone, from Buddha to the Beatles, says that all we need is love, maybe it's worth taking this piece of information seriously?

On the super scale (10 being super much), how much do you love:

a) yourself? ___/10
b) your life? ___/10
c) your job/career? ___/10
d) your close ones? ___/10
e) your world? ___/10
f) others? ___/10

How important would you say love is to you? How do you experience it? How do you show it? How do you distribute it? How often do you feel it? When? Where? Can you think of anything that's more significant than love?

I know, I know, too many questions at once, but I'm not asking these in order for you to answer them (not yet).

"Oh my friend, why do you care so much
for fame and prestige
when you neither think nor care
about wisdom and truth,
and the improvement of your soul?
Are you not ashamed?"
- Socrates

Socrates asked this question about 2500 years ago, and embarrassingly for us, it is still valid today. On a spiritual level, we haven't learned a lot since the ancient times. What would Socrates or any of our predecessors say if they travelled to the present day and saw what was happening? They wouldn't be able to deny all the progress we have made in our own right. Do you think they'd be proud of us because of our technological and scientific accomplishments? And what about the level of comfort we've reached? How do you think they'd react if they knew that, despite all this luxury, hygiene and freedom (in comparison to their times, at least) we're still unsatisfied, afraid and divided?

What/who's the human ideal according to you? ('why')

_____

_____

Is that ideal more elf or ogre-like? ('why')

_____

_____

Have you ever wondered why Socrates was considered the wisest man around at his time? Unlike many others, if he didn't know something, he asked questions, he observed, he did his research. We're all capable of doing that, aren't we?

"Life is really simple, but we insist on making it complicated."
- Confucius

"Simplicity is the ultimate sophistication."
- Leonardo da Vinci

"Get your thinking clean to make it simple. It's worth it in the end because once you get there, you can move mountains."
- Steve Jobs

The masterminds behind these three quotes certainly knew what they were talking about, right? So, with the con glasses off and no CG separation in sight, let's look into this 'simple' word. Simple means straightforward, uncomplicated, presenting no difficulty of any kind, easily said and/or done. On the super scale (10 being super simple), how simple/straightforward and uncomplicated are you towards yourself? ('why')

_____
_____

On the super scale (10 being super simple again), how simple/straightforward and uncomplicated are you towards those around you? ('why')

_____
_____

*"The ability to simplify means to eliminate the unnecessary
so that the necessary may speak."*
- Hans Hofmann

"If you can't explain it simply, you don't understand it well enough."
- Albert Einstein

PART NINE

Mankind isn't as complex as we might think. We get happy when someone is nice to us, we get sad when people are unkind to us. The small detail we seem to forget is that when we're the ones being unpleasant to someone else, it affects them the same way as it would us, regardless of whether we, or they, are right or wrong.

We're all trying our best, aren't we? Yet we're ashamed of our dark side and instead of being ourselves, we pretend we're more this or less that. Consequently, we fall right back into the con man/woman role. And how can we not? We're overwhelmed because of our society's imbalance between the matters of the body and the soul. It's hard not to feel anxious when the consuma greed crushes ethics and principles all around us, from the church to the government.

*"The day science begins to study non-physical phenomena,
it will make more progress in one decade
than in all the previous centuries of its existence."*
- Nikola Tesla

The civilisations before us were mystical. They paid attention to spirituality and respected The Divine. We've lost that side of Heavenly Reverence completely. In the consuma society, we think that it's 'silly talk' and that science has all the answers. Science, however, only has all the scientific answers.

> *"Science is only one of life's many languages*
> *communicating with us."*
> - Unanimous Anonymous

Meanwhile, nowadays our spiritual education is so weak to the point that mankind is corrupted no matter its beliefs, gender, skin colour or financial status. Our moral pendulum swings both ways. Thus, Volume One focuses on clearly distinguishing right from wrong so that we're able to use our free will correctly from now on.

> *"Whoever saves one life, saves the world entire."*
> - The Talmud (translated from Hebrew)

HUMANUAL A3

During his road to Enlightenment, Buddha was ready to do whatever it took to get there, including many extreme measures such as starvation. After he gave it a try, to the point of risking his life, that idea just seemed pointless to him. Why make yourself suffer more if we're all suffering already? How does that help us gain any insight? You can't focus when your mind and body are weakened by hunger and pain, can you?

His conclusion: "Moderation is key." Does it sound simple, obvious and logical? It is. Doing things in moderation means balancing between matters of the body and the soul as well as the elf versus the ogre ratio within.

> *"If you don't change direction,*
> *you may end up where you're heading."*
> *- Lao Tzu*

$$ELF + OGRE = HUMAN$$
$$ELF > OGRE = SUPERHUMAN = SUPERHERO$$
$$ELF < OGRE = SUPERVILLAIN$$

The truth is, we're all good and bad, elves and ogres. Each of us has the same buffet of temptations enticing us left and right, so it's good to see how well we are doing despite our shortcomings. Life is a rollercoaster (with ups and downs and Good Little Tests along the way) designed to challenge our resolve and character. Even The Hulk (Stan Lee and Jack Kirby credit), whose level of strength was normally proportionate to his level of anger, did his best to channel that anger for a good cause. He made mistakes along the way but overall did his best, even at his angriest.

Embracing and befriending both the light and the dark side helps you navigate through your solar (light, yang, male) and lunar (dark, yin, female) duality so that they resonate in tune with your soul.

Balance = successful living of the body + successful living of the soul

All superheroes represent your best potential and all supervillains represent your worst. Being a supervillain doesn't necessarily mean killing millions of innocent people, but it means using the four human superpowers (think, feel, say, do) for anything bad. Every single action of yours will be accounted for at the end of your life. However, we behave as if we don't care at all.

Whenever you find out that someone you don't like isn't doing well, how do you feel? Do you feel compassion for them or, if even for a second, that inner spark of ogre-joy? How about when you gossip about someone, do you ever wonder whether that behaviour is one of a superhero or a supervillain? Would you get +1 or -1 for that?

And when you witness someone being picked on (that awkward kid/person at your school/work, intimidated by fellow students/colleagues), please underline your most likely course of action:

a) defend the weak one   b) do nothing   c) join the bullying.

What would you say if a) you had an opportunity to make some quick and easy (yet dodgy) money, and b) you knew you'd never get caught?

YES / NO

"Who *wouldn't* say yes to easy money?" most people ask. I'll tell you who wouldn't: an honest person.

ONE LOVE + ONE TRUTH

Others can hurt your body, they can also hurt your feelings. No one except you, however, can ever hurt your soul, your true s(elf). The body is a vessel, a very impressive bio-machine for your soul, a piece of the divine nature. It's used to travel through the flow of the universe whilst living as a human and experiencing everything along the way. Everyone is in exactly the same boat here.

God, the Supreme Being, the Lord, the Source, the Spirit, Jahveh, Gaia, the Tao, Higher Self, Allah, Brahma, the Energy, Consciousness, the Chi, the Deity - they're all different names for One and The Same. Love, truth, faith, compassion, understanding, humility and respect are also part of One and The Same. God is a feeling, an unlimited energy (nature hasn't created limiting walls or borders). God equals It. Love equals It. Life equals It. Truth equals It. Nature equals it/It. Everything equals it/It.

Matters of the body (this world) = it / Matters of the soul (real life) = It

In this world 'it' means nothing really, the 'neither' nor the 'in-between', but in real life 'It' represents The Divine All, the No-Name (remember, words are man-made).

A Christian, a Jew and a Muslim focus on one human life, this life. A Hindu or a Buddhist focus on many lives. Together, they tell us the fuller spiritual story of creation. No single puzzle piece represents the entire image. In order for us to finally see the whole picture, we need to focus on putting all of the pieces together. Superheroes build bridges between each other, not walls.

What would a superhero choose here, a) become united or b) remain divided?

> *"The eternal difference between right and wrong*
> *does not fluctuate, it is immutable."*
> - Patrick Henry

> *"Alone we're strong,*
> *but together we're stronger."*
> - Sam Walton

THE SUPER SIMPLE MORAL COMPASS

There's far more that unites us than divides us, but don't forget that peace makes no money in the consuma society. It's important to question whether our political/spiritual leaders' values are superheroic or supervillainous. It becomes simple once you know what you're looking for. The only way to save humanity is through joint action of all individual human cells working together towards making Earth's body healthy again.

You choose your journey during which you balance matters of this world (body) and real life (soul). Whatever your decisions are, prepare for their consequences.

ACTION -> REACTION
CAUSE -> EFFECT

Life doesn't happen to you as a punishment. It happens for you as a gift. Your soul is hitchhiking in the body you've been assigned to see what you do with it, what you'll learn, and what your final score in this round will be on the superhero versus supervillain chart-board.

> *"We have two ears and one mouth*
> *so that we can listen twice as much as we speak."*
> - Epictetus

Thoughts are your soldiers and you're (meant to be) their general. All four human superpowers are supposed to follow your orders, as you're your body's leader and not the other way around. On the super scale (10 being super much), how much power/control do you have over your human apparatus? ('why')

_____

_____

A wise man speaks when he has something to say, a fool because he has to say something. If you think of your words and actions being tattooed and visible on your body for others to see, would you still be saying or doing the things you normally say and do?

YES / NO

"Logic is the beginning of wisdom, not the end."
- Leonard Nimoy

PART TEN

Logic is crucial to get you from A to B in an incorrupt manner. You should make use of it even if only to remind yourself not to make permanent decisions based on temporary emotions. Certain mistakes can't be unmade.

As for your place and the bigger meaning of your existence, apart from belonging to the Earth family, each one of us is an actual puzzle piece within the universal being's body, a cog within the living vessel, a part of One and The Same. Like a blood cell (both red and white) is part of your body, you are part of this Universal/Collective Consciousness. Our job is to make sure that life within It is healthy. We have a soul mission to do what we can to help It run smoother whilst building bridges between each other. You only become a brick in the wall if what you stand for is a message of division.

"Some people can read War and Peace
and come away thinking it's a simple adventure story.
Others can read the ingredients on a chewing gum wrapper
and unlock the secrets of the universe."
- Lex Luthor

"Logic will get you from A to B. Imagination will take you everywhere."
- Albert Einstein

"Reality is wrong. Dreams are for real."
- Tupac Shakur

On the super scale (10 being super important), how important would you say you feel in this world? ('why')

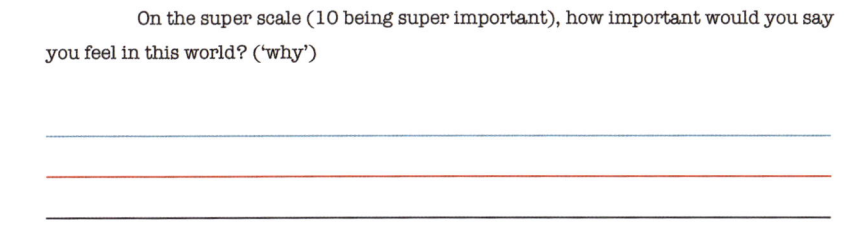

I'm asking you this in case you think it makes no difference whether you feel important or not. It does make a difference, a crucial one. Why? Because without you, the puzzle has a missing piece and therefore, is incomplete. You've got distinctive DNA, fingerprints, handwriting, signature and such, but that's not where your unique abilities end. There's nobody else with a mind and experiences like yours, which make you irreplaceable. Do you copy?

YES / NO

*"We all live with the objective of being happy.
Our lives are all different
and yet the same."*
- Anne Frank

Since reality is each individual's own perception of it, then mankind's reality is made up of our individual perceptions all put together into one collective human experience. Whether one of us imagines a flying machine, another one visualises a new theory, writes an article, makes a piece of music, a sculpture, a film, a website, a cure, a computer, an item of clothing, an engine or a wedding cake, they all (both good and bad, right and wrong) contribute towards the quality of our existence.

Your brain continually learns what you teach it. Teaching it about stress, doubt or regret doesn't seem like a comforting perception of human life, does it? Imagine if the great scientists, painters or entrepreneurs hadn't stretched their own minds into the new and unknown places with their brave ideas, thoughts and philosophies, if they hadn't dared to be different and curious, where would we be now?

> *"A man may die, nations may rise and fall,*
> *but an idea lives on."*
> - John F. Kennedy

Everything around you, as well as all the imaginary worlds, alternate realities, fairy lands, fantasy dimensions, games, melodies, poems, films, buildings, apps, tools, have all come to life right here, in this realm of ours, all born from our imagination. Aren't humans great? The power of the mind is measured by the depth of our beliefs. By believing strongly, we can even create miraculous recoveries, phantom pregnancies, placebo effects; we're that powerful. Unexplainable magic of all kinds happens when we allow our minds to run free and let the Universe work Its path.

Most of what goes on inside your mind stays there. Nobody has the slightest idea about the real you; your distinctive beliefs, hopes, dreams and anything else you can think of (literally). In our society, worrying takes up a great deal of our time. Most of the things we worry about never even happen, so imagine how much of our energy and despair is spent on something that isn't true...

Everyone else out there is also carrying this entire complex world within their own individual imaginations (don't judge a book by its cover). Now, multiply it by a few billion. The more individual human beings have happy experiences, the happier mankind becomes. It's not a 'maybe.' It's a certainty.

There's a difference between being busy and being productive, and in the consuma society, many are going nowhere and achieving nothing, fast. Yet, our dream of peace and unity is bigger than ourselves or our immediate needs, and it will take time to achieve. Therefore, before we even attempt to walk, we first need to learn how to crawl. The mission to save humanity requires your:

a) PATIENCE (quality over quantity)
b) PERSISTANCE (superheroes never give up).

At times, when happiness evades us, we've lost hope yet *still* try reaaally hard to make others happy, we may find we're unable to do so. Why is that? It could be because often, you can't give something you don't have. We hurt each other because we ourselves are hurting, off-loading some of our pain onto others, and so automatically adding -1s to our AND their suffering.

Size-wise, humans are limited. Our imagination isn't, though, and we've proven it time after time, civilisation after civilisation. Together we *can* create positive change.

The power of any master depends on the number of their followers, so in order for peace to win and become the world's master, we all need to act accordingly within the laws of peace. We can't *force* peace. We can only embody it.

Please take care of your mind and learn how to operate it because it is too powerful to be left unsupervised. In the control of the wrong person, it becomes a weapon of mass destruction, starting with you. Superheroics doesn't want to control your mind. It's here to free and protect it from those who do, for your imagination is a far greater superpower than the ability to fly, walk through walls or shoot laser beams from your eyes. Your imagination is how dreams come to life.

Scientifically speaking, all humans are made out of the same 'ingredients' as each other, even the same components as stars and planets, with all the tiny atoms flying everywhere, the waves, the energies, and so many other pieces that make up One and The Same. Let's add all of it into our reality's vision. Just because we can't see it, doesn't mean it's not there.

In order to save mankind, do you think you could put any of your remaining ogre-full opinions aside in order to work together towards a peaceful future? Only united, our puzzle pieces make a whole. We're far more inter-dependant on each other than we think. To remind you of what your true s(elf) already knows, you have all the ingredients, skills and talents you may need. Now you can take control of whichever dish of a life you cook for yourself. Feels good, doesn't It?

SUPERHERO CADETS = SPECTRAL LEAGUE = WARRIORS OF LOVE = ARMY OF ONE

Your soul is all about Its mission and Its calling. It's held back and can't move onwards and upwards unless you free It by freeing your mind. The Super Simple Moral Compass is the proven remedy for every superhero; real or imaginary. It's better than money too. Superheroics is a clear route towards unbreakable values that lead towards the light, together. It leads to a place where your words are true and your actions have purpose. Up until this very point, you've been a victim and a survivor, and now you have an option to let your soul become a warrior too. Equally, you can choose to do nothing and in ten years be exactly where you're at now, but a decade older.

Please picture my soul using my imagination as a tool to awaken yours. Cadet, are you there? Do you copy? HERE and NOW is where you choose to see this as:

a) just another story OR
b) an actual superhero cadet sending you a message in the shape of this book, reaching out to your soul (YES, **YOURS**) to help us initiate **all** the other cadets out there (you're surrounded by them), and help the superheroes win their final battle against the supervillains (beginning with your inner ones).

Remember that eyes can't see when the mind is blind. If the mind isn't switched on, the eyes become purely organ parts. The 'basic eyes' only have one mode, to merely notice the 'basic graphic design,' the superficial layer of reality. This is the simplest version of a human, in superheroics known as an 'OFF' or a 'zobot' (zombie + robot).

A real upgrade costs, but the currency isn't money. It costs everything except money; it costs time, work, effort, focus, strength, truth and love. It also costs **courage**, the first official super skill for the cadet to accomplish in order to be ready for Level Two.

How much are you willing to pay for happiness? Well, that depends on you. Are you prepared to brave the journey and to face the responsibility of your actions? Bear in mind that if one can do it, so can others.

MISSION FOR THE PRESENT:

1. Let your true s(elf) be known (both elf and ogre within).
2. Be inspired to take action, like they do in the movies. Right now, you're still at the beginning of your favourite film/book/tv series, where you're getting to know the characters. The lead character is a superhero cadet, so you root for them (in this case, you root for you).
3. Now that our paths have crossed, your super sidekick (me) and the superhero cadet (you) are about to head out on a big adventure to save mankind.

MISSION FOR THE FUTURE:

4. Press the switch of our Collective Consciousness (in superheroics It's called the 'super switch') ON

Side note: A group of aliens come across one of our space shuttle's remains floating about in the galaxy. Inside it, they find a variety of human movies and TV series. After watching them (and being impressed with the courage of mankind as portrayed in the stories), they decide to travel to Earth. They've just landed. What do they see?

Instead of meeting brave heroes, they come in contact with a hurting species. You can't put a 'filter' or a 'special effect' on truth. "That's the way of the world," we say. Correction. It's the choice of man because the world was in perfect harmony until we came along.

> *"Great acts are made*
> *of small deeds."*
> *- Lao Tzu*

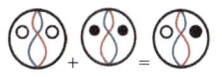

NEW BEGINNING

Where do we begin?

To counteract the Good Little Tests that we seem to often fail, we've got the Good Little Deeds to help us along the way. The GLDs are positive variables you can add into your daily equation at any point, starting from +1.

Had a bad day? At least you helped a friend with support/advice or a homeless person with a sandwich/spare change. To you it's not much, but to them it's everything. Mathematically, it may count as +1 only (this world), but giving someone time, hope and compassion is incalculable (real life). The Good Little Deeds also help raise our mathematical equation of the collective human experience with a few +1s here and there. That's how It all begins.

> *"Do not pray for an easy life,*
> *pray for the strength to endure a difficult one."*
> *- Bruce Lee*

Life is a range of situations and scenarios for us to experience, and learn from, to help us reach our full potential, since 'a smooth sea hasn't made a skilful sailor.' In whichever time and place you find yourself, growth is always happening at the end of your comfort zone. You're constantly obtaining s(elf)-awareness through the Good Little Tests placed on your path to Enlightenment.

What if you suddenly died now, would your soul be travelling North or South?

North / South

> *"Dead people receive more flowers than the living ones*
> *because regret is stronger than gratitude."*
> *- Anne Frank*

DEATH

"Some people meet death with open arms and thank God their time has come. Others beg to be spared for just one more day saying there is much to be done.

But if we, before performing an act, would stop and think of death
Of death, of judgment and of all such things
I'm sure we would do our best

So that when our time comes, we may say
Take me Lord without delay."
- Sister Cathy Cesnik

FINAL THOUGHTS... FOR NOW
2021

"Life can be so much broader, when you discover one simple fact,
that everything around which you call 'life'
was made up by people who were
no smarter than you."
- Steve Jobs

Every superhero story teaches us it's the superhero's incorruptible character, not their looks, money or status which matters in making the right choices, and that doing the wrong thing, no matter how 'small' it might seem on the supervillain scale, *never* works.

It also shows us that:
- there's no 'I' in 'TEAM'
- we're all equal
- anyone who has a will, *can* make a difference.

Words we use, as well as their meanings and concepts, are all man-made. As is fear. Nature knows no fear. All living beings, in fact, all *except* humans, know how to live in balance and harmony with each other, together creating a perfect whole. Mankind, however, fear-driven, entitled and greedy, keeps acting like supervillains, spoiling the life journey for everyone, from plants to animals, sea-creatures and more.

Superhero cadets know that evil is man-made too which, like cancer and/or a virus, has been spreading amongst us since the dawn of man when people chose to start doing the wrong things. In other words: No, it's not OK to hate, steal, kill, cheat, lie, betray or disrespect anyone, ever, in any way. That's the superhero ideal we should be striving for. Yet humans are committing evil like it's nothing as they stumble around in darkness, harming others in the process, blaming one another, judging, condemning, making the same mistakes repeatedly, generation after generation letting their egos run wild, acting like ogres whilst looking for a quick-fix to ease their pain. Why? Because the majority feel empty, without true hope or purpose, and can't see the light at the end of the tunnel.

It's as if mankind has been brainwashed into a self-destructive mass-psychosis of individuals who, no matter who they are, don't feel good enough. Mankind urgently needs a) hope and b) better idols than the current ones playing out on the world's stage. Looking at our leaders, one might wonder about their competence as well as the systems they represent. Doesn't it make you wonder why we shouldn't try something new instead, like the circle drawing exercise? Here's where *you* come in, if you want to, of course.

"Faulty tools produce faulty results."
- Jordan Peterson

Einstein said the definition of insanity is doing the same thing over and over again, and expecting different results. Do you really think then, that by electing the same people, just different names, whether based on their family ties, gender or skin colour, will make a difference? They want this charade to continue to keep you busy and distracted, not focused on what truly matters, which is our own liberty being under threat in these tumultuous times. If we keep voting for the same puppets and trusting the same organisations that peddled cigarettes and prescribed Thalidomide to pregnant women, and sold asbestos to the general populace, we'll get the same 'show' (that's all it is) over and over again, just different fashion trends and new ways of controlling us.

In life, like in tech, if you programme a computer in a faulty way, it will function in a faulty way. Therefore, if the new generations of mankind are kept being taught faulty data by the unenlightened older ones, they'll keep producing faulty results whether in their thoughts, feelings, words or actions. We need to upgrade the system of the Collective Consciousness urgently in order to reclaim Earth and defend the peace so clearly in danger, especially right now.

> *"Honesty is the first chapter*
> *in the book of wisdom."*
> - Thomas Jefferson

We can't expect a faulty and corrupt system to save us. We need to save ourselves. The difference between us, the oppressed, and our oppressors is that they're united and work together. We aren't, yet, but we're getting there, more and more of us rising and saying 'enough is enough.'

Saving the world doesn't have to mean huge gestures. What you say and do every day compounds over time. Same goes for the way you think and feel. If you're nice to one person a day, whether you give up your seat to an old person on the underground, help a neighbour with their groceries, smile at a stranger, text a friend asking how they're doing, that's 365 people per year whose lives you'd impact positively, and +365 points added to the equation of our existence.

The energy you put out into the world is the energy you create within your mind. What world are you creating within and around you, one of peace and possibilities or one of hurt and destruction?

*"Our lives begin to end the day we become silent
about things that matter."*
- Martin Luther King Jr.

The world is aching, and it needs our help. When Martin Luther King Jr. made his famous 'I have a dream' speech, do you think he envisioned the world as it is now?

We can't keep our heads in the sand hoping 'someone' will find a way. We have to *be* that someone. The rise of the global resistance is happening as you read this, The Great Rescue, Operation Earth 2.0. At this moment in history, you're presented with a choice. Which side are you on? Do you choose to act like a courageous superhero who heals and brings hope or a fearful supervillain who harms and brings pain? Please remember that what happens next is up to you.

*"Hope is the most precious gift you can ever give to another person.
Hope sparks faith, faith sparks action, action sparks change,
a positive domino effect that begins with a kind word."*

+

*"One day we'll all be nothing but a story.
Make sure yours is an uplifting one."*
- Czesław Słania

TO BE CONTINUED...

Website: superheroicsofficial.com
Instagram: @liv_s
Email: superheroicsofficial@gmail.com

Printed in Great Britain
by Amazon